CANADA'S FIRST PEOPLES

RON MUNRO

CANADA
A PEOPLE'S HISTORY

THOMSON NELSON

Australia Canada Mexico Singapore Spain United Kingdom United States

THOMSON
NELSON

Canada: A People's History
Canada's First Peoples

Series Consultants
Donald Bogle, Don Quinlan

Author
Ron Munro

Director of Publishing
Beverley Buxton

General Manager, Social Studies, Business Studies, and Languages
Carol Stokes

Publisher, Social Studies
Doug Panasis

Managing Editor, Development
Karin Fediw

Product Manager
Nadia McIlveen

Senior Editor
Loralee Case

Editorial Coordinator
Amy Hingston

Copy Editor/Indexer:
Penny Hozy

Executive Director, Content and Media Production
Renate McCloy

Director, Content and Media Production
Lisa Dimson

Production Manager
Cathy Deak

Senior Production Coordinator
Kathrine Pummell

Interior and Cover Design
Daniel Crack, Kinetics Design

Photo Research
Lisa Brant, Alene McNeill

Printer
Transcontinental Printing Inc.

Canadian Broadcasting Corporation Representative
Karen Bower

The authors and the publisher are grateful to the Canadian Broadcasting Corporation for its assistance in the preparation of this volume in the book series based on its 17-episode, bilingual television documentary series, *Canada: A People's History*. For more information about *Canada: A People's History*, please visit www.cbc.ca/history.

ISBN-13: 978-0-17-633653-0
ISBN-10: 0-17-633653-2

Printed and bound in Canada
3 4 09 08 07

For more information contact Nelson, 1120 Birchmount Road, Toronto, Ontario, M1K 5G4. Or you can visit our Internet site at http://www.nelson.com

To the Elders, who have maintained the knowledge and history of the great variety of Aboriginal cultures that exist across the Canadian landscape.

Contents

INTRODUCTION

THE BIG IDEA

Long ago, there were many diverse Aboriginal cultures living across Canada. They had lived here for as long as they could remember. Had they lived here since time began?

There are no written records to tell us about the early societies of the First Peoples. Yet we know a great deal about these ancient cultures. **Artifacts** left behind from earlier times tell us many things. We know about the housing in which people lived, the clothes they wore, and the tools they used. But there is much more to the past than material things. To learn about the cultures and values of the First Peoples, we must listen to the stories told by the **Elders**. These stories have been passed down from generation to generation. Over thousands of years, they have told the people about their past. They have contributed to their sense of community and have helped them preserve their cultural identity.

TIMELINE

63 000 BCE The last Ice Age begins

10 000 BCE Aboriginal peoples use sharp points and stone weapons to kill giant animals

9000 BCE The woolly mammoth and other big game become extinct

8000 BCE The last Ice Age ends

7000 BCE The First Peoples begin to develop a wider variety of tools and weapons

5500 BCE Maritimes First Nations develop burial mounds

5000 BCE The Plains Nations use corrals to kill large animals

The First Peoples had many different tools and technologies.

Picture This

Can you imagine what it would have been like to be the first people living in Canada? Imagine a world without grocery stores or shopping malls. Instead, imagine a world in which people depended on nature for their survival. What would it have been like to live in a tent made from tree bark or buffalo hides? What would it have been like to hunt and fish for food? Or to gather fresh fruits, berries, and nuts? What would it have been like to wear clothing made from plants and animal skins? What would it have been like to learn about your past from stories your people told you instead of from the pages of a history book? For thousands of years before Europeans came to North America, the First Peoples prospered in a world just like this.

TIMELINE

4000 BCE First Nations in the Great Lakes Lowlands use fish nets and weirs

1500 BCE Major trading networks begin to emerge

1000 BCE Various societies begin to develop pottery and stable village life

500 BCE Trade begins between First Nations in the Great Lakes Lowlands and the Atlantic coast

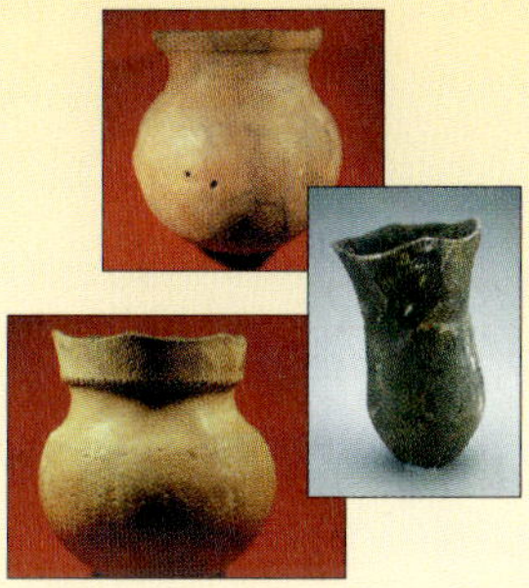

SETTING THE SCENE

The Peopling of the Americas

Aboriginal peoples were the first people to live in North America. No one is quite sure when or how they came here. Many historians believe they arrived sometime between 50 000 and 14 000 years ago. Most think they crossed over from Asia on an ancient land bridge that existed during the last Ice Age. Back then, **sea level** was much lower than it is today. This created a huge, grassy plain called Beringia. It connected Siberia with Alaska where the Bering Strait is today. Many people believe that the First Peoples crossed this bridge into North America as they followed herds of **migrating** animals.

Other historians think the First Peoples arrived here by boat across the Pacific. Some evidence suggests that they may have settled in Central and South America first. Later on, some of them migrated to North America. Other historians think that some of the First Peoples crossed the Atlantic Ocean to get here. They believe there is evidence that links these people to the early peoples of Europe.

Aboriginal peoples have another point of view, though. They believe they have lived here since time began. They have no connection to any other place. This is their homeland.

This photograph was taken in Beringia National Park in Siberia. It shows what the Beringia land bridge probably looked like thousands of years ago. Is this how the First Peoples came to North America?

TIMELINE

250 CE Aboriginal peoples begin to use bows and arrows for hunting

500 CE Maize is grown in the Great Lakes Lowlands

1000 CE The first known contact between Vikings and Inuit takes place in Newfoundland

1000 CE Beans, tobacco, and squash are grown in the Great Lakes Lowlands

1300 CE The Haudenosaunee (Iroquois) begin to build palisades around their villages

1400 CE As many as 2 million Aboriginal peoples occupy the land that is now Canada

This map shows possible routes that historians believe the First Peoples may have taken as they spread across the Americas.

TIMELINE

1450 CE The Iroquois Confederacy emerges as the most powerful political alliance in North America

1492 CE Italian explorer Christopher Columbus reaches the Caribbean

1523 CE French explorer Jacques Cartier establishes contact with Aboriginal peoples at the mouth of the St. Lawrence River

Living in Harmony with Nature

Long ago, millions of Aboriginal peoples lived all across North America. While there were many different cultural groups, they had a common **world view**. They believed that all people shared the land and its resources. Since they depended on nature for their survival, the people lived in harmony with it. They used the resources the world around them had to offer. But they never used more than they needed. They were careful to preserve things so they would be there for their children and grandchildren.

Yet while all Aboriginal peoples lived off the land, they did so in different ways. In the forests, the people hunted game and caught fish. They gathered wild plants and used the wood and bark of the birch tree to make many things they needed. On the prairies, the people relied almost totally on the buffalo. They used every part of the animal, for food, shelter, clothing, and tools. Nothing was wasted. Along the ocean shores, people survived on the bounty of the sea. They invented special hooks, spears, and nets to catch fish and other marine life. They used the trees of the dense forests to build shelters and canoes. In the north, seal and caribou were the most important animals. The people ate their meat and wore their hides as clothing. They learned to live in their icy environment by building shelters out of blocks of snow.

Telling Their Stories

THE EAST COAST STORYTELLER

Aboriginal **creation stories** tell of many different ways in which the earth and all its creatures came to be. The stories differ from culture to culture. Yet they all reveal the people's close spiritual connection with nature. Most share a common message about their origins, too: they believe they have been here since time began.

View the clip "Mosaic #1" (*Canada: A People's History*, Episode 1, 01:04:51 to 01:11:17). What do the creation stories of the Iroquois, the Haida, and the Blackfoot have in common? In what way does the story told by the West Coast Storyteller differ from the other stories?

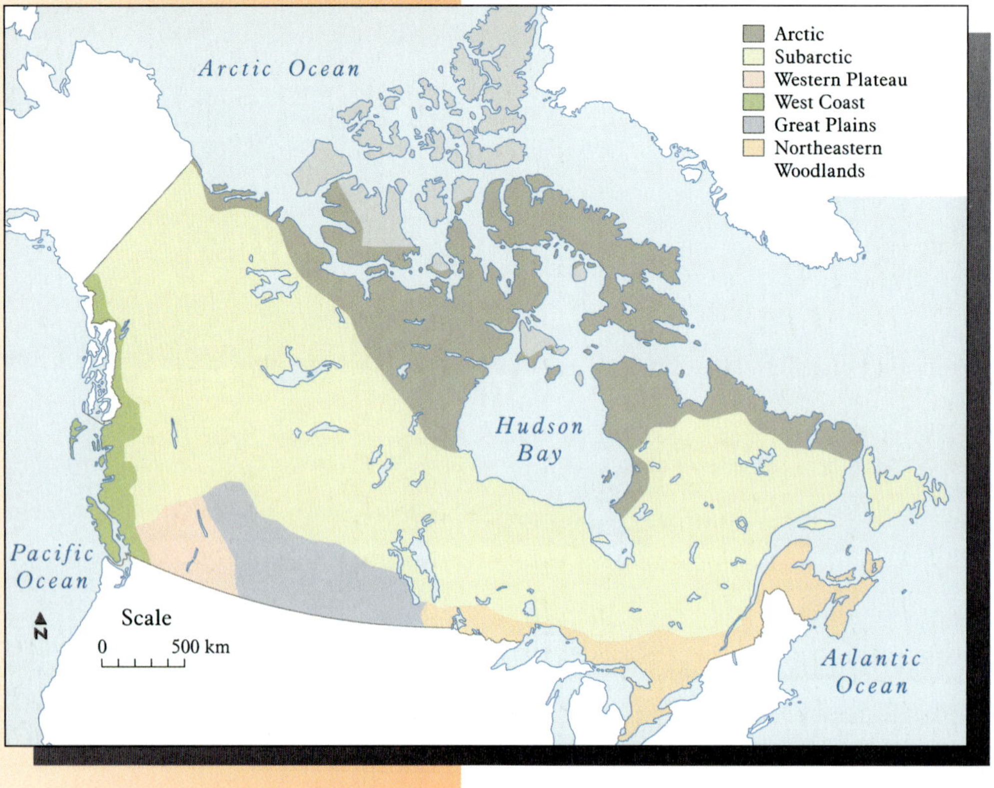

This map shows the physical regions of Canada in which different Aboriginal cultures lived.

A Culturally Diverse Land

The First Peoples created many distinct societies. Each culture was unique, with its own values and traditions. Long before Europeans knew it existed, North America was one of the most culturally **diverse** lands the world had ever known.

Canada's First Peoples focuses on the Aboriginal peoples who occupied the land we now call Canada before Europeans came. What were these early societies like? What were their cultural values and traditions? How did they preserve their cultural identities? How did they unite their communities? How did so many diverse peoples thrive in what was often a harsh and difficult land?

Playback

1. What did Aboriginal cultures in North America have in common? In what ways were they different?
2. How does the environment in which you live affect your way of life?
3. What are the different theories about when and how the First Peoples came to live in North America? Which theory do you think is correct? Why?

CHAPTER 1

THE ART OF STORYTELLING

One way to learn about people is to listen to the stories they tell. In Aboriginal societies, stories are very important. For thousands of years, Aboriginal peoples have kept their histories alive through the **myths** and **legends** they have passed down from generation to generation. These stories connect the people's past with their future. They tell how the people and their world came to be. They teach people knowledge and wisdom. They pass on spiritual values and morals. They teach important life skills. In this way, stories help to keep the traditions and way of life of Aboriginal peoples alive.

Throughout history, all civilizations have created stories to explain their world. These stories tell how the earth was created and how people and other living things came to be. This painting, called *Birth of the Earth*, shows a divine woman falling from the sky. With the help of the animals, the earth is created. It shows the connections Aboriginal peoples feel with nature. What creation stories does your culture tell?

Storytelling

Storytelling is a skillful art. Only a few respected Elders are chosen to be storytellers. In turn, they pass down this right to the next generation. Traditionally, certain stories were told at specific times of the year. Sometimes they were told to mark special occasions. Storytelling could last for a few hours or a few days. During the telling of stories, the people gathered to listen and learn and to enjoy each other's company.

Spirits of the Animal World

In the stories told by Aboriginal peoples, animals represent the spirits of the sky, earth, water, and sun. Animals such as bears, ravens, turtles, and coyotes have the ability to think, speak, and act like humans. They are creators, advisors, and spiritual guides. They deliver messages that help to guard and protect the people.

Raven is an important figure in many West Coast and Inuit cultures. Raven is full of supernatural powers. He has the ability to change himself from one creature into another. Sometimes Raven does this to trick people and other animals. Other times, though, he tries to help. In the story you are about to read, Raven coaxes the ancestors of the Haida Nation out of a clamshell on the beach to enter into his world peopled by birds, animals, and powerful creatures. This story reflects the Haida's belief that their roots are in the sea.

This artwork, by an Inuit artist named Kakulu Saggiaktok, is called *Ummajiit (Animals of All Kinds)*. It reflects the central role of animals in Aboriginal societies.

Raven was wandering on the beach, when he heard noise coming from a clamshell. He looked more closely and saw that it was full of little human creatures. They clearly looked terrified by Raven and the big world outside the shell. So Raven leaned his great head close to the shell and with the smooth trickster's tongue that had gotten him out of so many misadventures in his troubled and troublesome existence, he coaxed and cajoled and coerced the little creatures to come out and play in his wonderful shiny, new world.

— As told by Bill Reid, of the Haida Nation, at www.virtualmuseum.ca/exhibitions.Inuit_Haida

Other Transformers

Other Aboriginal cultures have a spirit similar to Raven. Among the people of the Plains and the Plateau, he is known as Coyote. The people of the Northeastern Woodlands know him as Glooscap. In parts of the Subarctic, he is known as Nanabush. The stories told in different Aboriginal cultures may share some common characteristics. But each story is unique and each has its own special meaning and purpose for the people.

Bill Reid, a Haida artist who lived in British Columbia, created this sculpture. How does it depict the story of Raven and the first Haida people?

Animals not only created the world. They helped the First Peoples to survive in their new land. When treated with respect, animals allowed themselves to be killed to provide food, shelter, and clothing for the people. Bears were particularly important animals to the Anishinabe, who lived in the Northeastern Woodlands. This story shows how bears hold a sacred place in their legends.

This painting is called *Bear Feeding.* The artist, Blake Debassige, created it to honour the importance of the bear in the Anishinabe culture.

For all their needs, the spirit woman and her children depended on the care and goodwill of the animals. The bears, wolves, foxes, deer, and beaver brought food and drink; the squirrels, weasels, raccoons, and cats offered toys and games; the robins, sparrows, chickadees, and loons sang and danced in the air; the butterflies, bees, and dragonflies made the children smile.... The bear, fearing the death of the infants, offered himself that they might live.

With the bear's sweet flesh, the infants survived. The death of the bear encompassed life for the new beings. Thereafter, the other animals sacrificed their lives for the good of men. When the infants grew to manhood and womanhood, they bore a special love for the bear and honoured him in their ceremonies. In gratitude and fondness they dedicated a prayer to the other animals.... Men and women survive and live because of the death of their elder brothers.

— From Basil Johnston, *Ojibway Heritage: The Ceremonies, Rituals, Songs, Dances, Prayers, and Legends of the Ojibway* (Toronto: McClelland & Steward, 1976), p. 16.

SPIRITS OF THE SKY

Many Aboriginal Nations tell stories about the sky spirits. These spirits help the people and teach them many important lessons. Their stories show the people how to respect all life and how to live together peacefully. Sometimes people die and become stars in the sky. Then the stars are always there to remind the people on earth how they should behave. This story, from the Plains culture, tells how the stars known in the Kainai Nation as the Wolf Trail (you may know it as the Milky Way) came to be. The Wolf Trail reminds the people of how the wolves taught them to survive.

Makoiyi (the wolves) were the first Ksahkomi tapiksi (Earth Beings) to pity us. One snowy winter, when our people were starving, a young man and his family camped by themselves as they searched for food. The wolves found the family and appeared to them as young men bringing fresh meat to their tipi. The wolves took this family with them back to their camp. There, there were many different animals camped together, and they helped the family to set up, make a fire, and get food. The animals shared many spiritual gifts with the man and also showed the man how to co-operate with other people when he hunted buffalo and other animals. The wolves also told our ancestors that animals with hoofs and horns were all right to eat, but that animals with paws and claws should be left alone. The wolves disappeared in the spring, but we still see them in the sky as Makoi-Yohosokoyi (Wolf Trail). These stars constantly remind us of how we should live together.

— As told by Rosie Day Rider and Louise Crop Eared Wolf of the Kainai Nation, at www.virtualmuseum.ca/Exhibitions/Cosmos/english/html/skystories.html

Translating Aboriginal Stories

Traditionally, Aboriginal stories were spoken aloud by the Elders in their native languages. The words and the way in which the storytellers expressed them had special meaning. Today, though, many non-Aboriginal people want to learn about these stories, too. This means that the stories have to be translated. Often, translating a story changes the meaning. So when you listen to an Aboriginal story told in your own language, remember that this is a *version* of the story. It is not the original story.

Sky spirits and symbols have traditionally been used to decorate tipis and clothing in the Plains cultures. This tipi from the Kainai Nation depicts a falling star.

Spirits Beneath the Deep

The icy waters of the Arctic are full of seals, whales, walruses, and fish. The Inuit depend on these creatures for their survival. Therefore, the most important spirit to the Inuit is Sedna, goddess of the sea. She rewards the people with a good harvest. Without her blessing, the people would starve. The story on page 13 tells how Sedna came to be and how she rules the seas.

Artists have created many different likenesses of Sedna. This stonecut and stencil is called *Sedna with Spotted Bird.* It was created by an Inuit artist named Lucy Quinnauyuak.

Long, long ago, when Sedna was a young girl, she refused suitors from her own clan. Instead, Sedna chose a mysterious lover who turned out to be a seabird in disguise. On hearing what had really happened, her father set out to rescue his rebellious daughter.

Finding Sedna in the nest of the seabird, he spirited her away. Father and daughter began the long journey home in a skin boat. The angry and abandoned seabird made a great storm to stop them. Fearing the great power of the seabird, the father decided to rid himself of his daughter. Sedna was thrown into the sea by her fearful father.

Trying to save herself, she grasped the sides of the boat, pleading with her father to pull her back into the boat. The selfish father, fearing for his own life, swung his knife, chopping off her fingers. Sedna soon sank below the waves and was gone. When Sedna's fingers fell into the water, the fingers became whales, seals, and polar bears [and] her nails became whalebone.

As the young woman sank into the sea, she was transformed into the mystical being known as Sedna, Mother of Oceans and ruler over all life in the sea. The blessings of Sedna are still sought by the people of the North who know it is She who sustains them.

— From www.spiralgoddess.com/Sedna.html

Telling Their Stories

SEDNA

There are many versions of the legend of Sedna. You can compare the story you have just read with another version told in *Canada: A People's History*. View the clip "Running Across the Sky" (*Canada: A People's History*, Episode 1, 01:28:39 to 01:29:45). How are the two stories similar? How are they different? Record your findings in a Venn diagram.

Playback

1. **What do each of the stories you have read in this chapter tell you about the beliefs of the First Peoples and their relationship with nature?**
2. **How do these stories compare with other creation stories you know?**
3. **Why do you think the meaning of a story might be changed through translation?**
4. **Think about a favourite story that you like to hear. Practise reciting this story. Then tell the story to the class.**

History in Action: Comparing Oral Histories

The Back Story
Aboriginal myths and legends have certain characteristics in common. They all tell something about the beliefs, values, and morals of a particular culture. Yet each story is different, too, and tells something about what makes each culture unique.

The Goal
In this activity, you are to compare and contrast two of the Aboriginal stories you have read in this chapter. Then you are to use your critical-thinking skills to prepare a reasoned argument.

The Steps
1. Reread two of the stories in this chapter. Then make a list of the key events and issues revealed in each one.
2. Complete a Venn diagram similar to the one shown here to compare the similarities and differences in the two stories.
3. Discuss the ways in which the stories provide insights into each Aboriginal culture.
4. Write a paragraph to support your point of view.

Evaluating Your Work
Think about the following criteria as you evaluate your work. Your work should:

- include a neat and carefully completed Venn diagram
- show evidence of critical thinking as you prepare a reasoned argument
- contain at least three points to support your point of view in your written work
- show your ability to use reasoned judgments to present your point of view

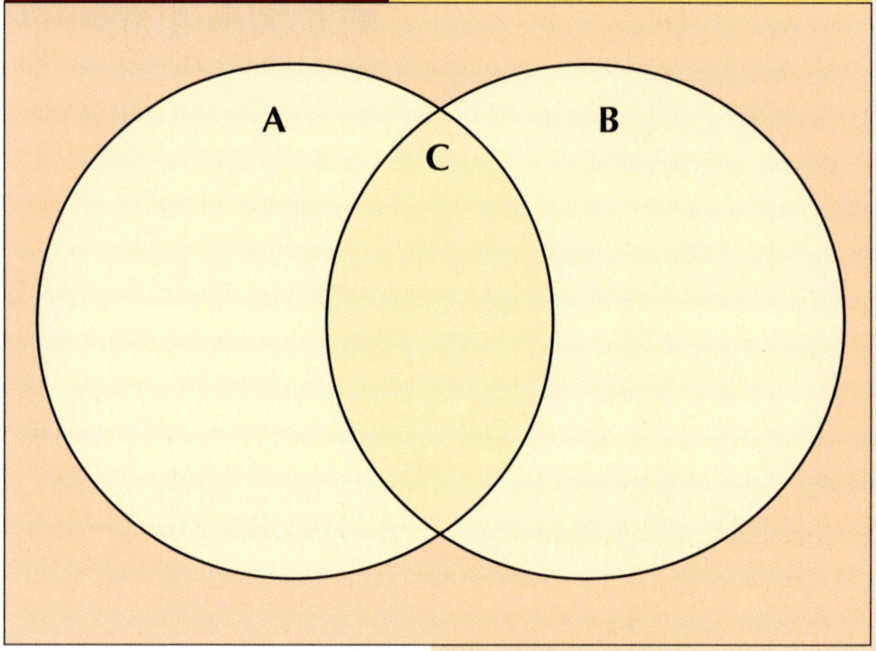

A Venn diagram is a visual way to compare and contrast information. Make a copy of this diagram. In space A, write the key points about one story in this chapter. In space B, write the key points about another story in this chapter. In space C, write those points that both stories have in common.

CHAPTER 2

PEOPLES OF THE NORTHEASTERN WOODLANDS AND THE GREAT PLAINS

These photographs show two different cultural environments. The photo on the left shows the Northeastern Woodlands. The other photo shows the Great Plains. Which environment do you think would have provided more resources for the First Peoples? What makes you think so?

The Northeastern Woodlands and the Great Plains are very different regions. As a result, the Aboriginal peoples who first lived in these regions developed different lifestyles and economies. The Northeastern Woodlands offered many natural resources to the First Peoples. These resources enabled them to be hunters, fishers, gatherers, and farmers. On the Great Plains, resources were more limited. The people depended on one resource in particular—the buffalo—for their survival.

Fishers and Farmers of the Northeastern Woodlands

Who Lived Here?

- **Beothuk**
- **Mi'kmaq**
- **Wuastukwiuk (*Maliseet*)***
- **Abenaki**
- **Haudenosaunee (*Iroquois*)**
- **Wendat (*Huron*)**
- **Attiwandaron (*Neutral*)**
- **Tionantati (*Tobacco*)**

***The names in italics are the European names for these Aboriginal societies.**

The Northeastern Woodlands stretch from the southern shores of the Gulf of St. Lawrence to the west of Lake Superior. In the days of the First Peoples, there was an abundant supply of vegetation and wildlife all across this land. There were deciduous trees, such as maple, oak, birch, elm, and beech. There were coniferous trees, such as spruce, pine, and hemlock. Shrubs and berry bushes were everywhere. The natural vegetation provided food to eat and materials to make clothing, shelters, and canoes.

Wildlife was everywhere, too. Moose, deer, beavers, otters, foxes, and rabbits were just a few of the animals that roamed freely through the forests. In the spring, summer, and fall, there were many migrating birds, such as ducks,

The climate is more hospitable in the Northeastern Woodlands than in most parts of Canada. Although winters are cold and snowy, they last only a few months. Summers, on the other hand, are longer and hotter than in most other regions.

geese, and pigeons. The lakes and rivers, too, were full of delicious fish, such as bass, pike, pickerel, trout, and perch.

Coastal Fishers and Hunters

The First Peoples living along the Atlantic Coast enjoyed an affluent lifestyle. The forests and oceans that surrounded them were abundant sources of food. The people lived their lives according to the seasons. As spring approached, they settled in villages along the coast. The village sites were carefully selected to be near the food supply. They may have been near shellfish beds or at the mouth of a river, where the people eagerly anticipated the first runs of salmon, herring, and sturgeon. They returned to these villages year after year and remained there until autumn.

In summer, the greatest source of food was the ocean. The people enjoyed a variety of shellfish, including scallops, mussels, oysters, and clams. They hunted the seals and walruses that came ashore to bask on the beaches in the warm sunlight. They fished for halibut, cod, and trout. Sometimes they hunted dolphin and small whales, too. They also used the rivers to travel inland on canoes, where they hunted game and gathered fruits and nuts.

In autumn, the people moved inland to avoid the coastal winter. They hunted game, such as moose, deer, bears, and otters. The meat from these large animals was preserved and stored to help the people survive the winter. At their winter villages, they covered their homes with fur skins for added warmth.

The Mi'kmaq developed a complex society. They adorned their clothing and containers with elaborate quillwork and they made sophisticated tools.

A Valuable Resource

Moose was important to the Mi'kmaq for more than just meat. The antlers, fur, and bones were used to make clothing, moccasins, bags, tools, and toys.

The Mi'kmaq built cone-shaped wigwams covered with birch bark. Sometimes they built larger, rectangular cabins for their extended families.

The coastal peoples had many seasonal celebrations. During these special times, it was important for the people to show their respect and give thanks for the animals. If they failed to do so, the soul of the dead animal would convey this to the other animals. Then the animals would become scarce and the people would starve.

People of the Longhouse

The Haudenosaunee (Iroquois) were the most powerful group of First Nations in North America. Once, these five nations battled among themselves. They were trapped in a cycle of death and destruction. Then, a legendary peace-maker named Dekanahwideh brought a message of peace to the people. He called it the Great Law of Peace. It was a code for living. It created laws for governing and taught the people how to behave in society. Dekanahwideh travelled throughout the Haudenosaunee territories, urging the people to form an **alliance** based on this new **constitution**.

Dekanahwideh succeeded in uniting the five nations in what became known as the Iroquois Confederacy. Each nation retained control over its own affairs. In matters of importance to the group, such as trade, treaties, and war, however, they met in a Grand Council. Chiefs were chosen to attend the meetings by the Clan Mother, who was the oldest woman in a clan. The chiefs consulted with their people so that their votes reflected the people's wishes. Decisions were reached by **consensus**. All nations had to agree before a vote was passed.

The symbol of the Iroquois Confederacy was the longhouse. In the villages, families related on the mother's side lived together in a large longhouse. Sometimes ten or more families lived in one house. Each family lived in a compartment on either side of a central corridor. They shared a central fire with the family on the other side of the hall. Above the door of each longhouse was the symbol of the family's clan. Each clan was named for the animal believed to be their original ancestor.

From the Sources

The Great Law of Peace was the unwritten constitution of the Iroquois Confederacy. The Elders passed down this law from one generation to another. Retelling the Great Law of Peace could take several days. The following written translation is a short excerpt.

The word that I bring is that all peoples shall love one another and live together in peace. This message has three parts: Righteousness and Health and Power... and each part has two branches.

Righteousness means justice practiced between men and between nations; it means also a desire to see justice prevail. Health means soundness of mind and body; it also means peace, for that is what comes when minds are sane and bodies are cared for.

Power means authority of law and custom, backed by such force as is necessary to make justice prevail; it means also religion, for justice enforced is the will of the Holder of the Heavens and has his sanction.

Dekanahwideh (left) and Hiawatha (centre) confront the Onondaga chief Atotarho, who was a fearsome wizard who opposed the alliance. Eventually, though, he agreed to join.

Farming led to permanent villages. As many as 1500 people lived in a village. The people built huge palisades around the villages to protect themselves from attack. Inside, they built platforms along the tops of the palisades. People stood on the platforms and shot arrows and dropped rocks on approaching enemies. The longhouses were made from poles carved from evergreen trees and covered with bark roofs. The roofs could be adjusted to suit changes in the weather.

Women held the power in the longhouse. The woman's family determined clan membership—if a woman was a member of the Bear clan, her children were members of the Bear clan, too. A man moved into his wife's longhouse and followed the rules of the eldest woman in the house.

Women held the power in the villages, too. Although men became the chiefs, the Clan Mother chose them. She held the balance of power. A Clan Mother could remove a chief from office and appoint a new chief if she believed he was not doing a good job.

The Haudenosaunee took advantage of the fertile soils and long growing season to farm. Men cleared the land for farming. Then the women took over. They were responsible for planting and tending the crops and bringing in the harvest.

The most important crops were corn, beans, and squash. The people planted corn and beans together in the same mound so that the corn stalks supported the climbing beans. Then they planted squash in between the mounds so that the leaves would discourage weeds. These three crops were so closely linked to one another that the people called them "the Three Sisters."

The First Farmers

The First Peoples knew a lot about farming. In fact, 60 percent of the crops grown today—including corn, squash, beans, potatoes, rice, turnips, tomatoes, and peppers—originated with Aboriginal peoples. In time, they would pass on their knowledge of farming to the rest of the world.

Playback

1. **The list on page 16 gives some of the traditional names of Aboriginal nations and the names that Europeans later gave them. Today, many Aboriginal peoples prefer to use their original names. Why do you think this is important?**
2. **The Iroquois Confederacy is the oldest** democracy **in North America. Describe the ways in which it is democratic. Then compare it with democracy in Canada today.**
3. **Prepare a fact sheet about one of the Aboriginal nations in the Northeastern Woodlands listed on page 16. Your fact sheet should highlight information about the nation's social structure, cultural traditions, and form of government.**

Who Lived Here?

- Anishinabe (*Salteaux*)*
- Nehiyawak (*Cree*)
- Nakoda (*Assiniboine*)
- Pikuni (*Peigan*)
- Kainai (*Blood*)
- Ah-ah-nee-in (*Gros Ventre*)
- Siksika (*Blackfoot*)
- Tsuu T'ina (*Sarsi*)

*The names in italics are the European names for these Aboriginal societies.

Hunters of the Great Plains

The Great Plains occupy a vast area across the centre of North America. In the east, tall prairie grasslands once covered these flat lands. Gradually, these tall grasses became shorter as the prairies stretched farther west. There were few trees on the plains, and few rivers, too.

The grasslands were a source of food to the millions of buffalo that once roamed the prairies. There were many other animals, too. Rabbits, prairie dogs, wolves, squirrels, ferrets, gophers, and coyotes lived alongside the buffalo herds. Hawks, eagles, buzzards, and owls were among the many bird species. In spring and fall, migratory birds such as whooping cranes, geese, and ducks stopped to rest during their journeys.

The climate of the Plains is extreme. Winters are long and cold. Blizzards can bring fierce, bitter winds and heavy snows. Summers are hot, but they are short and extremely dry.

The Bounty of the Buffalo

The people of the Great Plains built a lifestyle around the great herds of buffalo that roamed the prairies. Once, there were as many as 60 million buffalo. These animals were the single most important resource for the Plains peoples. They provided food, clothing, shelter, tools, and containers.

To hunt the buffalo, groups of extended families travelled together on foot across the prairies. They carried all of their possessions with them, with only their dogs as pack animals. With each season, the groups stopped to set up camps and to hunt, gather food, and hold celebrations.

Transportation was challenging for the Plains people. In summer, it was important to move quickly and easily as the buffalo herds moved on in search of fresh grazing land. The people built a carrying device called a travois to transport their children and personal belongings. A travois consisted of two long poles that were attached on either side of a sturdy net. Dogs pulled the travois across the dry grasslands.

Transportation was even more challenging in winter. The people built sleds to transport their belongings and wore snowshoes to travel across the snow. When there was time for fun and relaxation, they strapped on skates made from buffalo bones!

The Plains people developed two unique methods of hunting buffalo. In one method, several people lay hidden in the tall grasses in the formation of a V-shaped corridor. As the buffalo herds approached, they all jumped up, shouting and waving their arms. The frightened beasts stampeded down the human corridor into a makeshift corral. With the animals at close range, the hunters moved in for the kill.

Buffalo or Bison?

The term buffalo is commonly used to describe the great beasts of the Plains. They are also known as bison.

This illustration shows the Plains people and their dogs herding the buffalo toward a buffalo jump.

Waste Not, Want Not

For thousands of years, millions of buffalo roamed the Great Plains. These great beasts were the "supermarket" of the prairies! They provided the people with almost everything they needed to survive. No part of the animal was wasted.

The elk had power to influence matters of the heart.

The eagle was a symbol of vision and courage.

The second method of hunting was the buffalo jump. Once again, the hunters frightened the buffalo herds into a stampede. This time, they directed them toward the edge of a cliff. The terrified beasts plunged over the cliff to the ground below. Then the hunters' arrows and spears rained down on the stunned and injured animals.

Buffalo hunting required skill, patience, and cooperation. The rewards were great, though. A successful hunt yielded as many as 250 animals. This ensured that the people survived the harsh and bitter winter of the prairies.

The Power of the Animal Spirits

The Plains people had deep spiritual connections with the animal world. They believed that all animals were sources of supernatural power. Therefore, if they could attract these animal spirits to themselves, they could make them a force for good in their lives.

Traditionally, the people called upon the animal spirits during a **vision quest**. A vision quest helped a person prepare for a special time in his or her life. It could mark the passage from childhood to adulthood. It could signal the beginning or end of an important relationship. It could recognize a period of positive change or growth.

The bear was a symbol of courage in battle.

Telling Their Stories

BOY ON A VISION QUEST

A vision quest usually involved several days and nights alone in the wilderness. During this time, a person fasted and drank only water while saying prayers and waiting for a vision to appear. In time, an animal spirit appeared, as if in a dream. Speaking in a human voice, the animal spirit shared special songs and prayers as guidance for the person's life. Afterward, the spirit disappeared. But the animal remained sacred to the person for the rest of his or her life.

View the clip "Vision Quest" (*Canada: A People's History*, Episode 1, 01:22:12 to 01:24:48). How was the boy tested during the vision quest? What role was the boy given to play during his life? What warning does the Plains Storyteller give?

Playback

1. **What do you think would have been the most difficult thing about living on the Great Plains thousands of years ago?**
2. **Compare and contrast the lifestyles of the peoples of the Northeastern Woodlands and the Great Plains. In which environment would you have preferred to live? Give reasons for your answer.**
3. **After Europeans came to North America, the buffalo almost became extinct on the prairies. Do research to find out what factors led to the elimination of the great buffalo herds. Present your findings in a graphic organizer or a concept web.**

History in Action: Reaching a Consensus

Why is voting to reach a consensus an effective way to solve problems?

The Back Story

Reaching a consensus was an important method of decision making in many Aboriginal societies. It requires respect and cooperation among people and consideration for the benefit of the community rather than the individual. Consensus is one of the most democratic forms of government.

The Goal

Consider an issue affecting your class or school. Find a solution to this issue with your classmates by reaching a mutual agreement—that is, a consensus.

The Steps

1. Identify an issue in your school. Write the issue on the chalkboard.
2. Choose one student to chair a class discussion and another student to record notes on the chalkboard.
3. In the first phase, have a class discussion about the issue. Do not offer solutions at this time. Encourage everyone to participate.
4. In the second phase of the discussion, identify your concerns and express your opinion about the issue. Have another student record the key concerns on the chalkboard.
5. In the third phase, explore possible solutions to the issue. Discuss each idea carefully and record the key points on the chalkboard.
6. Once all aspects of the issue have been explored, propose a possible solution. Take a vote on the solution to see if there is a consensus. If there is not, discuss ways in which concerns might be addressed. Then hold another vote. A proposal can be adopted only if all members of the class agree to it. However, it is possible to reach a consensus even if some people still have concerns about the proposal. People can agree to disagree as long as they support the decision of the majority.

Evaluating Your Work

These are the criteria you should think about as you evaluate your participation in this activity. You should:

- share your ideas with the class
- listen when other students speak
- wait until others have finished before speaking
- ask questions when you do not understand something that was said
- disagree in a polite way
- treat everyone fairly

CHAPTER 3

PEOPLES OF THE WESTERN PLATEAU AND WEST COAST

Look at these photographs of the Western Plateau (left) and the West Coast regions. What do these regions appear to have in common? What appears to be different? How do you think the First Peoples who traditionally occupied these lands survived and prospered?

The land that is now British Columbia is the traditional home of two Aboriginal cultural groups: the peoples of the Western Plateau and the West Coast. Within each of these regions, there is a rich cultural heritage among many different nations. While they may have had some things in common, each nation was a distinct society. Each had its own customs, traditions, beliefs, and way of life. Each found a way to adapt to the conditions of their environment.

Who Lived Here?

- Tsilqot'in (*Chilcotin*)*
- Secwepemc (*Shuswap*)
- Stl'atl'imx (*Lillooet*)
- Nlaka'pamux (*Thompson/Couteau*)
- Okanagan
- Ktunaxa (*Kootenay*)
- Wet'suwet'en (*Carrier*)
- Tagish

*The names in italics are the European names for these Aboriginal societies.

Hunters and Fishers of the Western Plateau

The Western Plateau lies cradled between the Plains and the West Coast regions. It is a land of splendid scenery. In the north, there are high mountains and deep valleys. Farther south, the mountains are gentler and covered with thick coniferous forests. Glistening lakes often separate one mountain from another. Farther south still, rolling hills give way to sagebrush deserts.

Deer, elk, mountain goats, and bears were some of the wildlife that roamed the mountains and valleys. Eagles, hawks, and falcons swooped across the skies. Their steely eyes were always on the lookout for the most prized food of all: the salmon that filled the streams and rivers.

The climate of the Western Plateau is as extreme as the scenery. Northern winters are cold but dry. Moving south, temperatures gradually increase, but precipitation does not. In the southern tip of the region, summers are extremely hot and there is almost no rain at all.

The people of the Plateau borrowed traditions and customs from their neighbours. Like the Plains people, they were hunters. Like the West Coast peoples, they were fishers. They lived a **seminomadic** lifestyle. Between early spring and late fall, small family groups travelled from place to place. In spring, the men hunted game and waterfowl, such as beaver, rabbits, ducks, and geese. The women snared small game and gathered roots, bulbs, leaves, fruits, seeds, and nuts.

As summer arrived and the rivers began to fill with salmon, the people turned to fishing. With the arrival of fall, they began to plan for the winter ahead. They hunted large game, such as bear, deer, caribou, and mountain sheep. They preserved and stored the meat to eat during the winter. Then, as the weather turned cold, they gathered in their winter villages. The people continued to hunt for fresh game, such as deer, elk, and rabbits. Mostly, though, winter was a time for feasts and celebrations.

The Season of the Salmon

Salmon was an especially important source of food for many Plateau peoples. There were five different species of salmon. Each species returned to the same river at the same time each year to lay eggs, so the people always knew when and where to catch the fish. To show their respect for the salmon, some Plateau peoples held a special ceremony each year to welcome the first run of the season.

The people developed unique tools and technologies for catching salmon. At waterfalls, the fishers perched alongside the river's edge and used hooks, nets, spears, and basket traps to catch the fish. On narrow or shallow rivers, they built wooden weirs. A weir was a large fence made of tree branches placed together across a river. The fence trapped the fish, making it easy for the fishers to spear them. A good salmon weir could trap up to 1000 fish a day!

Preserving the Harvest

The salmon catch was rarely eaten fresh. Usually, the fish were cleaned and smoked over a slow fire. Then they were stored in underground pits lined with birch bark. Sometimes the people boiled the salmon in water heated with hot stones. When the water cooled, the oil rose to the top of the pot. They skimmed the hardened oil off the top and stored it in containers. Later on, in winter, they reheated the oil and mixed it with dried fish and saskatoon berries. This made a nutritious fish pemmican.

On most weirs, there was an opening so that some fish could pass through. Why do you think the people would want some of the salmon to get away?

During their solitary journeys, young people sometimes painted pictures on rocks. Today, archaeologists learn things about people's lives thousands of years ago from pictographs. These artifacts may be simple sticklike human figures. Or they may be complex drawings showing movement and technology.

Sacred Ceremonies

Winter was the time for games, storytelling, and spiritual celebrations. The Elders passed on the stories of their sacred traditions to the young. They taught them special songs about the spirit helpers. Sometimes, young people left the village to go on a vision quest. Alone in the wilderness, they sought the guidance of a spirit helper. The spirit helper provided people with their unique identities. It also gave them special skills, such as hunting, healing, and weaving.

Winter was also the time for ceremonial dances. Some dances were to protect the people from evil spirits. Others were to promote peace and harmony. Most plateau societies were democratic. There were no class distinctions. Every family was equal to one another. Women were equal to men. In fact, in some societies, Elder women were believed to have greater wisdom than Elder men.

Playback

1. What do you think would be the most difficult aspect of a seminomadic lifestyle? Give reasons for your answer.
2. Sketch a rock art drawing to tell about a typical event in your daily life.
3. Do some research to find out more about one of the cultures of the Western Plateau and create a visual presentation of your findings.

Fishers of the West Coast

The West Coast is a land of mountains and beaches, islands and fiords, lakes and rivers. Dense forests cover much of the land. Although the soil was not good for farming, the natural environment provided the First Peoples with a year-round garden. Everything they needed was available to them in the rainforests or the ocean waters. Along the shores, the people gathered shellfish such as clams and mussels and caught fish such as cod, halibut, and salmon. On the ocean waters, they hunted marine mammals such as seals, sea lions, and sea otters.

On land, the people gathered fruits, nuts, berries, and gull eggs. From the dense forests, they obtained one of their most valuable resources: the giant cedar. They used cedar logs to build their homes and canoes and cedar bark fibres to weave their clothing and blankets.

Who Lived Here?

- **Tlingit**
- **Nisga'a *(Tsimshian)****
- **Gitxsan *(Tsimshian)***
- **Tsimshian**
- **Haida**
- **Heiltsuk (*Bella Bella*)**
- **Nuxalk (*Bella Coola*)**
- **Oweekeno (*Kwakiutl*)**
- **Kwakwaka'wakw (*Kwakiutl*)**
- **Coast Salish**
- **Nuu-chah-nulth (*Nootka*)**

***The names in italics are the European names for these Aboriginal societies.**

The climate of the West Coast is extremely wet. The rains are often heavy. The temperatures are mild, though. Winters are not too cold, while summers are not too hot.

Since food was so readily available, the people of the West Coast had more leisure time than other Aboriginal cultures. They used much of this free time to create art. Because they lived in permanent communities, they created art on a grand scale. Beautifully decorated houses, majestic canoes, and colourful totem poles were all ways in which the people expressed themselves through art.

Water transportation was essential along the West Coast. The Haida were known for their magnificent canoes. Neighbouring nations were eager to trade goods for Haida canoes. Decorations on the canoes reflected the supernatural powers of the animal spirits or lessons learned through spiritual encounters.

Telling Their Stories

CEREMONIAL TOTEM POLES

Every Aboriginal nation had its own unique arts and technologies. The people developed these in response to the resources that were available to them. Many of these arts and technologies have been practised for thousands of years. Over time, cultures came to be known for certain skills and characteristics.

View the clip "Mosaic #3" (*Canada: A People's History*, Episode 1, 01:49:11 to 01:51:16). What can you learn about different cultures from these scenes? What do these scenes tell you about the diversity of cultures that existed thousands of years ago?

Tales of the Totem Poles

The art of the totem pole was unique to the West Coast. In fact, only six First Nations traditionally carved totem poles: the Nisga'a, the Haida, the Kwakwaka'wakw, the Nuxalk, the Tlingit, and the Coast Salish.

Totem poles were a way for the people to tell the stories of their families and clans. A totem pole proudly displayed the family crest, such as a raven, eagle, bear, beaver, or killer whale. The carvings beneath the crests recorded the family's important relationships, accomplishments, and adventures. In this way, the totem poles preserved the people's histories.

Trade Among Nations

The West Coast Nations and the Plateau Nations had a well-established trade network. The Plateau peoples traded tanned skins, goat wool, and dried berries for seashells and dugout canoes from the West Coast peoples. A prized trading item for the Plateau peoples was dentalium shells. These shells were found only in certain places along the coast. People used the shells to make jewellery and decorate clothing. All Aboriginal groups valued the shells and they became a form of money.

The people of the West Coast knew that cedar was full of natural oils that helped to preserve the wood. Therefore, they used these trees to carve their totem poles and preserve their family stories for future generations.

From the Sources

The West Coast peoples have a rich artistic heritage. The abundance of natural resources and the ease in harvesting them meant that people had more time to create art.

Art was one with culture. Art was our only written language. It documented our progress as a people, it documented the histories of the families. Throughout our history, it has been the art that has kept our spirit alive.

— Haida artist Robert Davidson, in M. Ian Thom, ed., *Eagle of the Dawn*, (Vancouver: Vancouver Art Gallery, 1993), p. 8.

Killer whales have a large fin on their back.

Raven crests have straight beaks and eagle crests have sharp, curved beaks.

Bears and beavers have ears on the tops of their head.

Beavers have two large front teeth as well as ears.

There were different housing styles in West Coast communities. The styles depended on the particular nation and their location in the region.

West Coast Villages

The West Coast peoples lived in villages along the coast. A village consisted of several large houses made from giant cedar planks. Houses were arranged in rows along the shore, with the entrances facing the water. Each house had its own history and its own name, such as "House Which Thunder Rolls Across" and "House That Other Chiefs Peer at from a Distance." What do you think these names mean?

The West Coast cultures had a social system that was different from other Aboriginal societies. There was a distinct class structure. At the highest level were the chiefs. Typically, a chief led between 150 and 200 people within his clan. The clan included the immediate family, an extended family, adopted members, and slaves. At the second-highest social level were the nobles. They inherited their social standing. Beneath the nobles were the commoners. They were the hunters, fishers, artists, and traders in the clan. At the lowest level were the slaves. Slaves were captives from other nations or people who had fallen into debt and had lost their social status. Slaves had no rights within the community. Their status was passed down from generation to generation.

Within this social system was an economy based on **private ownership**. Social standing reflected a person's wealth. The more a person owned, the higher the social standing. But unlike modern concepts of wealth, West Coast peoples believed that true wealth lay in how many goods people could give to others rather than how many goods they could keep for themselves. The traditional **potlatch** reflected these values.

The Pride of the Potlatch

The potlatch was a special celebration of family pride in West Coast cultures. It marked an important event in the life of a chief, such as a birth, a death, or a marriage. Guests at the potlatch were invited to witness the event.

At a potlatch, the host family gave gifts to all those who attended. Food, blankets, artwork, cedar chests, shell jewellery, fishing rights—even slaves were among the gifts bestowed. The more lavish the gift-giving, the greater the social honour the chief received.

A family spent years making and collecting gifts for a potlatch. Once the potlatch began, it lasted for days or even weeks. Everyone in the community took part. There were stories, feasts, songs, and dances. When it was over, it was up to the high-ranking guests at the potlatch to return the host's generosity. Their potlatches were expected to be even more lavish than the previous one. If they failed to live up to this expectation, they were shamed. In this way, potlatch ceremonies distributed wealth and resources to everyone in the community.

This artwork re-creates a Kwakwaka'wakw potlatch ceremony of feasting and gift giving.

Playback

1. **In what ways did the environment influence the artistic expression of the West Coast peoples?**
2. **What animals are associated with some of your cultural celebrations?**
3. **Do further research on West Coast totem poles and explain the meaning behind the animal crests shown in this section.**
4. **In which of the two regions in this chapter would you have preferred to live? Give reasons for your answer.**

History in Action: A Family Totem Pole

The Back Story

Totem poles display the symbols and stories of a family or clan. They are similar to a family coat of arms. The clan or family emblem appears at the top of a totem pole. Beneath this emblem are images of important events and relationships in the family's life.

The Goal

Think about what makes your family special. Then choose an animal, bird, or fish to represent your family as you create a unique family crest.

The Steps

1. Reflect on your family's history and those things that make your family special. Write down brief notes about any special stories in your family's past.
2. Think of an animal, fish, or bird that reminds you of your family or that has something in common with your family.
3. Use the animal, fish, or bird you have chosen as the symbol for a family crest. On a separate piece of paper, design and illustrate your family crest. You may use photographs to guide you, but make your design an original.
4. Now pick three or four key events from the past that you would include on a totem pole about your family.
5. Illustrate each of these family events on separate pieces of paper. Then tape or paste all your pieces of art together to create a totem pole. Begin with the family crest at the top. Then place each event in order beneath the crest.
6. Once you have completed your totem pole, present it to the class as you explain your family story.

In what ways do artistic traditions help to preserve a culture?

Evaluating Your Work

These are the criteria you should think about as you complete your work. Your work should:

- include an original design for a family crest
- reveal three or four key events in your family's history
- be colourful and creative

Chapter 4

Peoples of the Subarctic and Arctic

These two photographs show the northernmost regions of Canada—the Subarctic (left) and the Arctic. What do you think these regions have in common? In what ways are these regions different from one another?

The Subarctic and Arctic peoples faced some of nature's harshest challenges. To survive, they learned to be wise and skilful hunters. They developed the tools and technologies they needed to survive and prosper in the most difficult environments in North America.

Hunters of the Subarctic

In the north, the Subarctic is an enormous region. It stretches from the coast of Labrador in the east across to the Pacific in the west. In the south, dense forests of spruce and fir abound. Moving north, the forests gradually give way to patches of smaller trees. Then small shrubs replace the trees, until finally the Subarctic becomes open **tundra**.

The First Peoples survived by hunting and fishing. Big game, such as caribou, moose, and bears, were the most valuable catches. There were many smaller mammals, too, such as beavers, otters, minks, squirrels, marmots, and lynxes. Ducks, geese, eagles, gulls, and terns were also in abundance. The many streams and lakes provided pike, trout, pickerel, and whitefish.

Who Lived Here?

- Innu
- Nehiyawak (*Cree*)*
- Algonquin
- Chipewyan
- Dunne-za (*Beaver*)
- Dakelh (*Carrier*)
- Wet'suwet'en (*Carrier*)
- Sekani
- Dene-thah (*Slavey*)
- Dogrib
- Kaska
- Tahltan
- Tagish
- Tlingit
- Tutchone (*Tuchone*)
- Han
- Hare
- Kuchin

*The names in italics are the European names for these Aboriginal societies.

The Subarctic climate is extreme. Winters are long and cold. Temperatures are usually below zero, and snow often falls in September and lasts until May. Summers are short, but the days are filled with sunlight, warm temperatures, and flowing waters.

This beautiful coat was made from caribou hides. After the hides were tanned, they were stitched together with animal sinew. Extracts from berries, bark, and other natural materials were used to paint the design.

People of the Trail

Many different cultures lived in the Subarctic region. Their lives were closely connected to the animals that roamed this vast land. The people moved in family bands through the woodland trails, tracking moose, bear, and caribou. In summer, they set up camps along the lakes and rivers. Food was plentiful. The people hunted, fished, and gathered plants and berries. Large groups of related families came together to share games, feasts, songs, and dances.

Summer did not last long, however. By early fall, the first snowfall marked the beginning of the long, cold winter. Now the people divided into smaller family hunting groups. Each group travelled to find its own territory—one that was large enough to supply food to survive the winter. Groups were free to hunt and fish where they wished. They never crossed into each other's territories, though. They knew they had to leave enough animals in a territory to breed so there would be more game in the years ahead.

Respect for the Spirits

Animals had an important place in the peoples' beliefs, stories, and ceremonies. Like many Aboriginal cultures, young people went alone into the forest on a vision quest. There they would wait to be contacted by an animal spirit. The spirit would give them special knowledge and power. While on their quest, the Subarctic peoples learned to read the trails to track animals.

Keeping Count

Aboriginal peoples knew that hunting depended on skill and knowledge—not luck! They studied the animals in their territory carefully to learn their habits and life cycles. They kept count of the number of animals so they would know when it was time to move to new hunting grounds.

When large game animals were scarce, the people snared smaller game, such as rabbits, porcupines, and muskrats. As the winter wore on, however, these animals often became scarce, too. The people then relied on dried fish and meat as well as pemmican, which they had stored for the winter. Still, people sometimes faced starvation as they waited for spring and the new bounty it would bring.

Tracking the Caribou

Each spring, the caribou began their annual migration in search of fresh grazing land. Hunters gathered in wait along their migration routes. Caribou was as important to many Subarctic peoples as buffalo was to the Plains peoples. Caribou meat was the **staple** of their diet. Caribou hides were made into clothing, moccasins, and tents. Caribou leather was fashioned into snares, fishing nets, and snowshoes. Caribou bones and antlers became fishhooks, knives, and other tools.

Caribou were hunted in corrals, similar to those the Plains people used to hunt buffalo. The people built a

The Algonquin peoples invented the canoe. Travel across many parts of the Subarctic would have been difficult without these vessels.

long fence in the shape of a funnel. At the end of the fence was a corral. When the hunters found caribou, they herded them into the funnel, down the corridor, and into the corral. Then, they shot the animals with their bows and arrows.

People often travelled on foot. In summer, they placed packs on their dogs to carry their personal belongings. Where there was a network of waterways, the people built lightweight, birch-bark canoes. They carried the canoes between bodies of water. The canoes allowed the people to travel long distances easily and quickly.

For winter travel, the people invented snowshoes. With snowshoes, they could walk across the deep winter snow without sinking into it. They built toboggans to transport food and other supplies.

Homes were built with the materials that were available at each new campsite. Most homes were cone-shaped, using wooden poles joined at the top and covered with birch bark or animal fur. While homes varied according to location, the camps were always set up in a similar way. The rising sun was the symbol of good fortune, so the entranceway for the houses always faced the early morning rays of the sun.

Playback

1. **What do you think would have been the most difficult thing about living in the Subarctic thousands of years ago?**
2. **Look at an atlas map of Canada. Why was it important for the Subarctic peoples to invent a convenient form of water transportation?**
3. **Aboriginal peoples made snowshoes out of different materials and in different shapes and sizes. Find out more about the snowshoes used in the Subarctic. Prepare a poster showing pictures or drawings of different types of snowshoes.**

Who Lived Here?

- Inuvialuit
- Copper Inuit
- Caribou Inuit
- Netsilik Inuit
- Iglulik Inuit
- Labrador Inuit

FISHERS AND HUNTERS OF THE ARCTIC

Of all the regions on earth, the Arctic is perhaps the harshest environment in which to live. Much of the land is a windswept polar desert for nine months of the year. Yet the Arctic is a very beautiful place, too. In the north, there are mountainous islands ringed with deep fiords. In the summer, melting snows create lake-studded lowlands. There are no trees in the Arctic, but in places with enough moisture, low-lying plants abound. Where it is dry, the land is barren and rocky.

There were fewer game animals in the Arctic than in other regions. The First Peoples relied on animals that had adapted to the cold, such as caribou, seals, polar bears, walruses, and musk oxen, to meet their needs. An abundance of Arctic char, cod, and trout provided them with fresh fish. Terns, ducks, geese, and golden plovers were among the many birds that migrated north each summer.

Arctic winters are long and extremely cold. Summers are cool and very short. In the far north, there are days in the winter when the sun never rises—there is no daylight at all! In the summer, the opposite happens. The sun never sets and it is daylight all the time.

Living in the Arctic was challenging. Yet for the Inuit it was possible not only to survive but to thrive in the icy landscape. In summer, they travelled in small family groups hunting caribou, musk oxen, wolves, foxes, and bears. Huge flocks of ducks, geese, and other waterfowl filled the skies and waters. On the coast, the Inuit gathered shellfish and berries and went out to sea to catch fish and marine animals. They moved frequently, returning to their favourite places each year. They didn't build permanent villages, though.

The Inuit sometimes hunted polar bears. They had to be careful, though — the bears were not afraid of them. In fact, sometimes the hunters became the hunted! Inuit hunters often circled back

Telling Their Stories

INUIT HUNTERS

The Arctic presented a challenge to the people who lived there. In this frigid, icy world, the forces of nature were always at work. The people learned to understand these forces and to find the best ways they could to survive.

View the clip "Musk-Ox Hunt" (*Canada: A People's History*, Episode 1, 01:29:50 to 01:30:42). What does this scene tell you about the way of life of the people who lived in the Arctic? What is the narrator referring to when he says "islands of subsistence in a universe of ice"? What do you think would be the hardest part of living in this environment?

Animal Spirits

Like all Aboriginal peoples, the Inuit had a special connection with animals. They held special ceremonies to ensure a successful hunt and to honour the animals that were killed. To ward off evil spirits, the Inuit wore religious charms made from animal parts, such as owl claws and caribou ears.

Strategies for Survival

As their world turned to ice, Inuit families headed out to sea. For several months, they lived in small **iglu** villages built on top of the ice that covered the ocean. There, they hunted one of their prized resources—ringed seals. Inuit hunters waited at the seals' breathing holes. When the seals came up through the holes for air, they quickly harpooned them.

At the end of the day, the hunters returned to the villages with their catch. The Inuit used every part of the animal. They ate the meat, blubber, and internal organs, which were rich in vitamins. They burned oil made from the blubber to create heat and light. They made the tough, waterproof seal skins into boots and buckets.

This picture of an Inuit family was taken in 1903. Life in an iglu then was similar to life in an iglu long ago. The family sat on ice platforms covered with skins for warmth while food simmered in a pot over seal-oil lamps.

Inuit Ingenuity

The Inuit found many ways to adapt to their environment. They created many unique inventions. During the winter, the Inuit built snow houses called iglus. Blocks of hard snow were built from the inside up to create a dome-shaped dwelling. At the top, they cut a hole for ventilation. The entranceway was cut lower than the floor inside. This kept the warm air in and the cold air out. Iglus came in many sizes. Some were a single room. Others were built with passageways connecting several rooms.

The Inuit learned to build their iglus quickly. It took only about an hour for two people to build a small iglu.

Inuit parkas were made of caribou hides trimmed with animal fur. They were designed to fit snuggly around the neck. Drawstrings around the sleeves and bottom sealed a person inside and kept body warmth in the parka. Men's parkas had small hoods attached to them. Women's parkas had larger hoods designed to carry

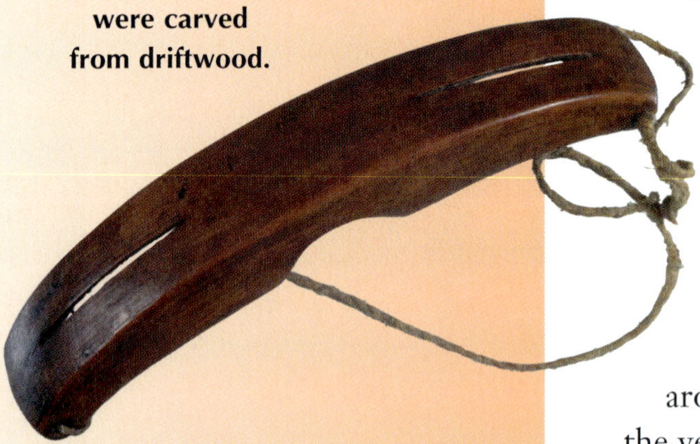

These snow goggles were carved from driftwood.

To protect their eyes, the Inuit created special snow goggles. Without them, the bright sunlight shining on the snow and ice would cause them to go blind. The goggles were made of narrow pieces of wood or ivory. Slits were cut in the centre so the person wearing the goggles could see.

A kayak was a slender, lightweight boat for one person. It was made from skins stretched over a frame. In a kayak, the hunter attached his parka around the opening, sealing himself inside and making the vessel watertight and unsinkable.

If a kayak overturned, the hunter used his oars to flip it back up again. This made it possible to travel in winds and rough waves.

The Inuit used kayaks to hunt marine animals and sea birds.

A umiak was a broader, flat-bottomed boat used to transport families and supplies. It could carry as many as 20 passengers at a time. During the hunting season, the Inuit used umiaks to hunt whales. They paddled up close to a whale to harpoon it. Floats attached to the harpoon prevented the whale from diving beneath the water. The hunters had to be careful, though. A single sweep of a whale's flippers or tail could smash a umiak to pieces!

When a umiak was used to move families, women rowed the boat while the men steered with a paddle.

The Inuit were skilled craftspeople, too. They designed and made all of the tools and utensils they needed in their daily lives. In spite of the hardships of Arctic life, the people found time to create crafts, such as pottery, masks, baskets, and jewellery.

With the vast, open tundra stretching across the horizon, the Inuit needed guideposts to help them find their way. They built stone markers called inuksuks. The word means "that which stands in for a man." An inuksuk had many purposes. It could show direction, point the way to good hunting grounds, or warn of danger ahead.

Carving was a skill the people used every day to make pots and bowls. Some carvers made simple sculptures, too, using ivory, stones, and bones.

Inuksuks were sturdy enough to withstand the fierce winds and heavy snows that often swept across the Arctic landscape.

Playback

1. **With a partner, brainstorm some of the ways people might adapt to long periods of daylight and darkness.**
2. **In a group, discuss the ways in which the Arctic environment affected the type of food, clothing, and shelter the people had. Record your ideas in a visual web.**
3. **Think about the Inuit inventions you have read about in this section. Which one do you think was the most valuable to the people in their daily lives? Give**

History in Action
Comparing Environments

The Back Story
For thousands of years, Aboriginal peoples lived all across the land that is now Canada. The plants and animals supplied the people with their basic needs. The landscape and climate determined their technologies. Different peoples faced different kinds of challenges. Yet they all found ways to overcome them and survive in this northern land.

The Goal
Working with a partner, create a graphic organizer to compare the environments and cultures discussed in Chapters 2, 3, and 4. Then, choose one environment and make an illustrative collage to show what it was like in the early days of the First Peoples.

Criteria \ Cultures	Wood-lands	Plains	Plateau	West Coast	Sub-arctic	Arctic
Physical Features						
Plants and Animals						
Climate						
Shelter						
Tools and Technologies						

Use a graphic organizer similar to this one to compare the cultures and environments of the First Peoples.

The Steps
1. With your partner, review each chapter by taking turns reading the text aloud. While one person is reading, the other should take point-form notes about physical features, plants and animals, climate, shelter, and tools and technology.
2. When you have taken notes for each environment, fill in the comparison organizer. You can make your own copy of the organizer shown here or you can create your own.
3. With your partner, choose one environment and culture to be the subject of your collage. Using the notes from your organizer, draw pictures or find photographs or illustrations you can photocopy or download from the Internet to illustrate this environment and culture.
4. Decide on a way to organize and present your collage. Be sure to include labels for your pictures.
5. Present your finished product to the class.

Evaluating Your Work
Think about the following criteria as you complete your work. Your work should:
- include a completed comparison organizer showing the six different cultural environments
- include a collage to illustrate the characteristics of one environment, with accurate visuals and labels
- be neat and complete
- be attractively designed and presented

CHAPTER 5

FAST FORWARD

Today, members of some First Nations in British Columbia take a Tribal Journey each year. Travelling by canoe, they retrace the routes their ancestors travelled. Along the way, they follow the ancient protocols of their people. As they enter a new territory, a speaker from each canoe announces their arrival. He or she then asks permission to come ashore. On shore, the people greet them with a special ceremony. How do you think this journey helps the people keep connections to their past?

The First Peoples in North America prospered for thousands of years. With the arrival of Europeans in the 1500s, however, their lives changed forever. At first, the First Peoples shared the land with the Europeans. They taught them how to survive in the wilderness. They helped them build new lives in a strange land. Soon, however, the Europeans began to dominate both the land and the people who lived there. As they did, the long-standing partnership

Some Aboriginal Inventions

Long before Europeans came to North America, Aboriginal peoples had invented many things. We still use some of these things today. Here are a few examples. Do you know of any others?

- Thousands of years ago, First Nations were the first people to grow corn. They even knew how to heat the kernels to make popcorn! Today, corn is a common crop grown all over the world.
- Chewing gum was an Aboriginal invention. The sweet, sticky gum was collected from spruce trees.
- Aboriginal peoples discovered that willow trees contained an ingredient that relieved pain. Today, this ingredient is used in many common painkillers.
- Aboriginal peoples invented canoes and kayaks. Today, many people use these boats for fishing, transportation, and fun!
- Aboriginal peoples invented Canada's official national sport, lacrosse. Some people believe that Canada's unofficial national sport—hockey—developed from lacrosse.

CONTACT AND CHANGE

Contact with Europeans was deadly for Aboriginal peoples. The newcomers brought diseases that were unknown in North America. The First Peoples had no **immunity** to these illnesses. As a result, thousands died. Entire communities—sometimes entire nations—were wiped out.

European settlement also disrupted Aboriginal societies. Nations were forced off their lands as settlers moved further inland. Then Canada became a nation in 1867. The new country wanted to open up the west to settlers. To do so, it needed to build a railway across the prairies to the Pacific Ocean.

The Plains First Nations knew they could not stop the coming changes. So instead, they tried to preserve their societies. Through **treaties**, they agreed to live on **reserves**. In exchange, the government made promises to help them build a new way of life. But the promises were never kept. The First Peoples found themselves struggling to survive in a land that had once sustained them. Their communities grew weaker. As they did, it became harder to keep their cultures strong.

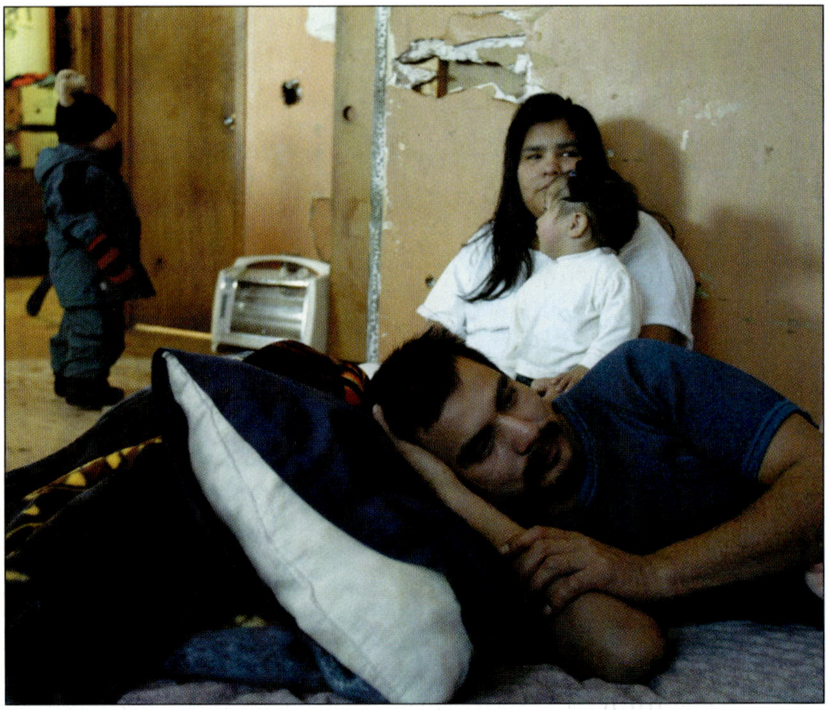

This family lives on a reserve in Rapid Lake, Quebec. The photo reveals the housing crisis on Aboriginal reserves in Canada today.

RENEWING ABORIGINAL SOCIETIES

In the twentieth century, Canada began to flourish as a nation. But Aboriginal societies continued to decline. For years, they struggled to keep their traditions and cultures alive.

Then, around 1970, a change began to take place. Like women and other groups, Aboriginal peoples began to demand equal rights. A cultural **renewal** began to take place. The First Peoples demanded greater control over their lives. They demanded that their rights be recognized and respected. They began the process of renewing their traditions and restoring their cultures. They set out to build a better future for themselves.

LANDS AND RESOURCES

Aboriginal peoples have always gained their sense of identity from the land. Their traditional activities helped to define them as a people. Today, the First Peoples want to renew their identities. They want to regain control over some of their traditional lands. They want places where they can build new spiritual and cultural homes. They want land where they can build local economies based on traditional activities such as hunting and fishing. They want equal opportunities to benefit from natural resources through industries such as logging and mining.

To achieve these goals, many Aboriginal groups have entered into talks with the government to settle **land claims**. Some groups have reached landmark agreements. Two of these were the Nisga'a agreement in 1998 and the creation of Nunavut in 1999.

The Nisga'a agreement in British Columbia gave the people **self-government** and $253 million. They also received the rights to forest and mineral resources as well as hunting and fishing rights. In return, the Nisga'a gave up any further land claims.

In 1999, the creation of Nunavut was the largest land settlement in Canada's history. The new territory is huge—2 million square kilometres. The Inuit own 18

The Indian Act

In 1876, Canada passed the Indian Act. The act defined who was a member of a First Nation. It gave the government control over the lives of all First Nations peoples. The act was used for many purposes. It banned traditional ceremonies such as the **potlatch.** It forced Aboriginal children to attend **residential schools.** It controlled activities on the reserves. It denied Aboriginal peoples the right to vote.

From the Sources

In some parts of Canada, Aboriginal peoples never signed any treaties or agreements with the Canadian government. Therefore, they believe they have the right to their traditional lands.

I guess the white man calls it "land claims".... But the term really describes how they came and took our land without consulting us, doing away with Aboriginal people in the millions. But we survived. And today, we are still in our land.... It belongs to our grandfathers and grandmothers. We never signed anything away.

— Ayuukhl Nisga'a, *Nisga'a: Peoples of the Nass River* (Vancouver: Douglas and McIntyre, 1993)

In addition, the Inuit received $1 billion in cash. In return, they gave up any further land claims.

There are still many other land claims to settle, though. Many of these claims involve small groups of people scattered across the country. It is harder for these groups to keep up the pressure on the government to settle their claims. Still, it is likely that there will be many more land settlements in the future.

Nisga'a leaders arrived at the land claim talks in a ceremonial canoe. Why do you think they did this?

The territory of Nunavut makes up 20 percent of Canada. The Inuit have occupied this vast land for thousands of years. Nunavut means "Our Land" in the Inuit language of Inuktitut.

SELF-GOVERNMENT

Many Aboriginal peoples believe that land claims go hand-in-hand with self-government. They believe the case for self-government is a simple one. They were here first. Each society lived as an independent nation. Each nation was self-governing. When Europeans arrived, the First Peoples were forced to submit to their laws and their governments. Yet they never gave up their status as nations. Therefore, their history gives them the **inherent** right to govern themselves.

Aboriginal leaders believe they should have **jurisdiction** over their own lands and people. They want to create their own justice systems, schools, health care systems, and businesses. They want to take charge of their own futures.

The Canadian government has other ideas about self-government, though. It agrees that Aboriginal peoples should have the right to control some things, such as schools and local economies. But it disagrees about the right to control other matters, such as justice and health

In 1999, women and children staged a peaceful demonstration

From the Sources

When Europeans first came to North America, they knew Aboriginal societies were independent nations. In time, though, they came to believe they had the right to govern the land and all the people who lived there. Today, Aboriginal peoples want to regain the right to govern themselves.

We all believe…that as First Nations we should have our own governments with jurisdiction over our own lands and people.

We should decide about and benefit from the type of development we want in our own territories….

We should have tribal courts run by our own people. We should [run] our own child-care and social services. We should take control over our own education….

Provinces would no longer have authority over us in our own lands, and whenever federal-provincial agreements were negotiated, we would be [given] a role similar to that of provinces today…. [We] would be regarded as a third participant, a separate founding nation, exercising control over its own territories

— Georges Erasmus, past Grand Chief of the Assembly of First Nations, in Boyce Richardson, ed., *Drumbeat: Anger and Renewal in Indian Country* (Toronto: Summerhill, 1989), pp. 2-3.

care. Today, the issue is still being discussed. In the future, perhaps new leaders and new governments will come up with new ideas that will satisfy both sides.

The Royal Commission on Aboriginal Peoples

In 1996, the Royal Commission on Aboriginal Peoples published a report. It included some ideas about how self-government should work.

The report said that:

- self-government should apply to Aboriginal nations rather than single communities
- a House of First Peoples should be created that would be equal to the federal and provincial governments
- Aboriginal peoples should have dual citizenship as citizens of both Canada and their Aboriginal nation
- Aboriginal nations should have the right to vote on their own constitution and laws

What do you think about these ideas?

Renewing Aboriginal Cultures

Traditionally, the family was at the centre of Aboriginal societies. Children, parents, and grandparents lived together. They maintained close ties with their clans. Then, in the first half of the twentieth century, the government tried to **assimilate** Aboriginal peoples into Canadian society. Children were sent to live in residential schools. Some children were adopted or placed in **foster care**. Poverty on the reserves forced young people to move to the cities to find jobs. Celebrations such as the potlatch were banned. All of these things made Aboriginal cultures weaker than they had been.

Elders are the keepers of traditional knowledge. They hand down the songs, stories, and ways of doing things to young people. They connect them to their history, culture, languages, values, and traditions.

$1.00 YEAR 32 • NUMBER 25 • JULY 23, 2004

NUNATSIAQ NEWS

Iqaluit's budget crunch
Homeowners don't want to pay for it — 5

Tourist tally
Business slow in Nunavut this summer — 3

Tanya Tagaq Gillis of Cambridge Bay, who toured with Icelandic pop star Björk in 2001, performing last week at Riddu Riddu, a Sámi music festival in Arctic Norway, with Origami Arktika, an acoustic rock band from Oslo. Gillis's music combines traditional throat-singing with contemporary pop and folk music. (PHOTO BY STEIN BERNTZEN)

Liberals' Newfoundland man defends Nunavut fishery

"The wrong information is out there," Efford declares at scrum in Iqaluit

JIM BELL

The Liberal government's political minister for Newfoundland, John Efford, this week defended the Baffin Fisheries Coalition and how it plans to develop Nunavut's 100 per cent turbot allocation in northern Davis Strait, saying "absolutely false information" lies behind recent allegations that the BFC is giving Canadian fish to foreigners.

"I want to see the people adjacent to the resource benefit from the resource," Efford said at a scrum organized for reporters in Iqaluit this past Monday.

The Liberal MP for Bonavista-Trinity-Conception, Efford is also Canada's minister of natural resources and the federal Liberal party's political boss for Newfoundland. He co-chaired this week's energy and mines meeting at Inuksuk High School.

Efford said he took time out that morning for an interview on CBC radio in St. John's — with Nunavut MP Nancy Karetak-Lindell — to clarify a CBC St. John's story that aired

LIBERALS'...4

Arctic adventure ends
Hiker drowns in Auyuittuq Park — 3

Kids on wheels
Skate park brings new toys to town — 6

INSIDE

Nunavut	3
Op-Ed	12
Letters	12
Jobs/Tenders	19

Publications Mail Agreement # 40068998
www.nunatsiaq.com

Many communities publish newspapers and magazines in their native languages. The *Nunatsiaq News* in Nunavut is published in the Inuit language of Inuktitut and in English.

Reclaiming Sacred Objects

One way Aboriginal peoples are making their cultures strong again is by reclaiming their artifacts. Many objects on display in museums are sacred to the cultures that created them. Many people believe these objects should be returned to their owners. Some museums have agreed and have returned the artifacts. Others want to keep the artifacts, but they allow the people to use them for special ceremonies. What do you think? Should these artifacts be returned to the nation that created them?

Today, Aboriginal peoples are making their cultures strong again. They are using their traditional names. They are working to make sure their languages survive. They are renewing family values. They are celebrating age-old ceremonies. They are expressing their cultures through music, art, dance, and literature. In what ways do the

In 1993, the National Aboriginal Achievement Awards were created. They honour the work of Aboriginal peoples in many fields, such as arts and culture, business, education, and sports. The awards help to build pride in Aboriginal communities.

Today, Aboriginal peoples celebrate potlatches and pow-wows with new enthusiasm. Events like the annual Curve Lake Pow-wow in Ontario renew spiritual and social ties. These ceremonies have changed over the years. But they still maintain the traditions and values of the people.

In 1996, Canada created National Aboriginal Day. It is celebrated on June 21 each year. The date is important to Aboriginal peoples. It is the longest day of the year, which is a traditional day of celebration. National Aboriginal Day honours Aboriginal peoples. Celebrations include pow-wows, games, feasts, storytelling, and dancing.

A GALLERY OF

Art has always had an important place in Aboriginal cultures. It reflects their attitudes toward their societies. It reveals their respect for the beauty and bounty of nature. It expresses their connections with the spiritual world.

In the twentieth century, however, the old ways of expressing art were lost or forgotten. Then, in the 1950s, a group of artists began teaching themselves the symbols and crafts of the past. They combined traditional methods with modern symbols and new materials. By the 1980s, these artists had created many unique and distinct art styles. They became leaders in the renewal of Aboriginal cultures.

Since then, interest in Aboriginal art has spread throughout Canada and around the world. People of many backgrounds have come to appreciate the beauty, quality, and variety of art created by Aboriginal artists.

Robert Davidson is one of the leading artists in the renewal of West Coast Haida art and culture. He is a master carver of totem poles and masks. In 1969, he raised the first new totem pole in the Queen Charlotte Islands since the potlatch was banned in 1884. Today, Davidson is one of Canada's greatest artists. His work is seen around the world. This display is called *Three Variations on Killer Whale Myths*. These totem poles are part of an exhibit of the world's greatest sculptors. They are on display on the grounds of an international company in New York state.

ABORIGINAL ART

Daphne Odjig is an Odawa artist. She was one of the artists who led the cultural renewal in the 1970s. This painting is called *Indian in Transition.* It reflects the cultural changes that have taken place in Aboriginal societies. Odjig has received the *Order of Canada* for her work. She has also received the highest honour from her home reserve—an eagle feather. In the past, only great male hunters and warriors received this feather.

Kenojuak Ashevak, an Inuit artist, created this print, made with felt pen on woven paper. It is called *The Owl.* Inuit artists, printmakers, and sculptors are famous around the world. Ashevak is a member of a group of women artists in Cape Dorset in the Northwest Territories. She uses modern methods and materials to create traditional Inuit art styles. Collectors around the world eagerly seek the work

A GALLERY OF

Kingmeata Etidlooie was an important artist in the Cape Dorset art community before her death in 1988. This acrylic painting is called *Spirits Emerge*. It shows the artist's deep connections to the spiritual and animal worlds. Etidlooie's works are on display in many major collections, including the Canadian Museum of Civilization and the National Gallery of Canada.

Aboriginal Art

David Ruben Piqtoukun from the Western Arctic has been creating sculptures for over 30 years. Many Inuit artists are famous for their sculptures, particularly soapstone carvings. This carving is made from Brazilian soapstone and caribou antler. It is called *Voyage of the Spirit-Helpers.* It reflects the artist's Inuit traditions and heritage. Piqtoukun's sculptures are on display around the world, including a huge sculpture in the People's Sculpture Park in China.

Playback

1. Do you think that Aboriginal peoples have an inherent right to govern themselves? Give reasons for your answer.
2. In a group, discuss ways in which people celebrate their culture and history.
3. In Aboriginal cultures, traditional knowledge is passed down from one generation to another. What knowledge about your culture do you think you will pass down when you are older?
4. Do research to find out about the life and work of one well-known Aboriginal person. It could be someone in politics, the arts, sports, business, or any other field. When you have completed your research, write a biography highlighting this person's achievements.

History in Action: An Aboriginal Art Gallery

This artwork, by Sarni Pootoogook, is called *Dancing Spirits.* What do you think you can learn about a culture through its art?

The Back Story

Today, many Aboriginal artists are inspired by their legends, spiritual beliefs, and traditions. They use their art to embrace their cultural identities. They also use art to address current issues that affect Aboriginal societies. Many of these artists still rely on traditional methods and symbols from the past. They combine these with images and symbols from today's world. What do you think you can learn about a culture through its art?

The Goal

Produce your own Aboriginal art gallery using photocopies from books or images from the Internet of Aboriginal paintings, sculptures, and/or carvings.

The Steps

1. Using information from this book and other resources, make a list of different Aboriginal art forms. Then decide on a theme for an Aboriginal art gallery. For instance, you may want to focus on Inuit or West Coast art or on a type of art, such as painting or sculpture.
2. Collect appropriate books from the library resource centre and/or use the Internet to find examples of Aboriginal art for your art gallery. Photocopy or download possible choices to include in your gallery. Be sure your selections are in colour.
3. For each selection, record the following information: the name of the artist, the cultural group to which the artist belongs, the title of the piece of art, and the type of media the art is, such as a soapstone sculpture or a woodcarving.
4. Choose five pieces of art to include in your art gallery. Then prepare a poster to present your choices. Be sure to include the reference information beneath each piece of art.
5. Present your art gallery to the class. Describe each piece of art in your own words. Then, as a class, discuss the message each piece of art conveys.

Evaluating Your Work

These are the criteria you should think about as you complete your work. Your work should:

- have a focus or theme
- include clean colour photocopies from art books or downloaded art images from the Internet
- provide reference information for each piece of art
- be visually appealing

Glossary

alliance a friendly agreement between groups

archaeologist a person who studies the past by looking at remains left at historic sites

artifact an object made by human activity

assimilate to make a minority group of people practice the customs of a larger group

consensus a general agreement of opinion

constitution the set of rules that govern a nation

creation story the beliefs a people have about how they came to be on earth

democracy a nation where the government is elected by the people

diverse varied or different

Elder a senior person in Aboriginal society who preserves and passes on the people's traditional knowledge

foster care to live in a family relationship with people who are not one's birth or adoptive family

immunity the ability to resist disease

inherent existing as a permanent attribute

jurisdiction legal authority

land claim a legal claim by an Aboriginal group over the right to use an area of land

legend a traditional story that may or may not be accurate or true

migrating moving from one place to another

myth a traditional story that usually involves an imaginary or supernatural character

Order of Canada an order of merit to honour Canadians for their special achievements

potlatch a celebration in some Aboriginal

pow-wow a cultural gathering that takes place in some Aboriginal societies

private ownership ownership by an individual for personal gain and benefit

protocol the rules of a procedure or group of people

renewal the process of restoring something to its original state

reserve an area of land set aside for use by an Aboriginal group

residential school a boarding school once run by the church or the government for Aboriginal students

sea level the average level of the sea's surface

self-government government of a group by its own people

seminomadic to occasionally move from one place to another

staple a raw material such as fish, wheat, or timber

translate to express words in another language

treaty a legal agreement between nations

tundra a flat, treeless region in the Arctic with a marshy surface

vision quest a sacred ceremony in some Aboriginal societies in which a person goes to a secluded place to communicate with the spirit world

world view a group's view of the world and its relationship to it

Index

Credits

Cover: Top: Ian Martens/CP Photo Archives; bottom left: CBC, Canada: A People's History; bottom right: Ted S. Warren/CP Photo Archives; Page 2 Top to bottom: National Park Service, © Katerina Wessels, National Archives of Canada, c-114467, Glenbow Archives, ND-3-6777; Page 3 Left: National Archives of Canada, c-09767, Right: Canadian Museum of Civilization, Bottom: National Park Service, © Katerina Wessels; Page 4: The Three Sisters, Ernest Smith, Rochester Museum & Science Center (MR 1014); Page 5: Newberry Library, Chicago; Page 7: Birth of the Earth by Arnold Jacobs/Two Turtle Studio; Page 8: Ummajiit, stonecut/stencil, 1995 by Kakulu Saggiaktok. Reproduced with the permission of the West Baffin Eskimo Cooperative Ltd, Cape Dorset, Nunavut; Page 9: Raven and The First Men by Bill Reid, Museum of Anthropology, UBC, N61.481; Page 10: Bear Feeding by Blake Debassige, McMichael Canadian Art Collection, 1975.40.4. Reprinted by permission of the artist; Page 11: Glenbow Archives, NA-1241-869; Page 12: Sedna with Spotted Bird, stonecut/stencil, 1982 by Lucy Quinnauyuak. Reproduced with the permission of West Baffin Eskimo Cooperative Ltd, Cape Dorset, Nunavt; Page 15 Left: © Mike Dobel/Masterfile, Right: Darwin Wiggett/firstlight.ca; Page 16: Victoria Hurst/firstlight.ca; Page 17: McCord Museum, M973.85.6A; Page 18: Indian Camp, New Brunswick by William Robert Herries, The Beaverbrook Art Gallery; Page 19: Newberry Library, Chicago; Page 20: National Archives of Canada, c-09767; Page 21: The Three Sisters, Ernest Smith, Rochester Museum & Science Center (MR 1014); Page 22: Kitchen-Hurst/firstlight.ca; Page 23 Top: Don Schimmel/MaXx Images, Bottom: National Archives of Canada, c-114467; Page 24 clockwise: Glenbow Archives, NA-812-8, Glenbow Archives, NA-2084-64, Glenbow Archives, NA-812-13; Page 25: CBC; Canada; A People's History; Page 26: Tannis Toohey/Toronto Star; Page 27 Left: Victor Last/Geographic Visual Aids, Right: Darwin Wiggett/firstlight.ca; Page 28: Darwin Wiggett/firstlight.ca; Page 29: National Archives of Canada, c-65097; Page 30: Gary Braasch/CORBIS/MAGMA; Page 31: David Nunuk/firstlight.ca; Page 32: Canadian Museum of Civilization; Page 33: Glenbow Archives, NA-1141-14; Page 34 Top: Glenbow Archives, NA-1700-56, Bottom: AA 1746; Kwakwaka'wakw Headdress, mid-20th c; wood, metal, paint; H: 31cm x L: 26cm x W:22 cm. Collection of Glenbow Museum; Page 35 Top: Canadian Museum of Civilization. Reprinted by permission of the Bill Reid Foundation, Bottom left: Collected on Haida Gwaii in 1879 by Israel W. Powell, CMC VII-B-1054 (S92-4297), Bottom right: Acquired from Chief Henry Wiah of Masset in 1901 by Charles F. Newcombe, CMC VII-B-1130 (S92-4407); Page 36: Courtesy of the artist, Gordon Miller; Page 37: National Archives of Canada, c-74693; Page 38: © J.A. Kraulis/Masterfile; Page 39 Left: T. Allofs/Masterfile, Right: John Foster/Masterfile; Page 40: Janet Foster/Masterfile; Page 41: Naskapi Caribou Coat, Royal Ontario Museum, 916.22.9; Page 42: Canada Museum of Civilization; Page 44: Sherman Hines/Masterfile; Page 45: Mike Macri/Masterfile; Page 46: National Archives of Canada, c-024522; Page 47 Top: Thomas Fisher Rare Book Library, P10032, Bottom: Glenbow Archives, NC-1-546c; Page 48 Top to bottom: Canadian Museum of Civilization; Page 49 Top: Canadian Museum of Civilization, Bottom: Brian Summers/firstlight.ca; Page 51 Left: Ted S. Warren/CP Photo Archive, Right: Ted S. Warren/CP Photo Archive; Page 52: Johnathan Hayward/CP Photo Archive; Page 54: Ray Smith/CP Photo Archive; Page 55: Andrew Vaughan/CP Photo Archive; Page 56: © Lyn Hancock; Page 57: Courtesy of Nunatsiaq News; Page 58 Top: Courtesy of NAAA, Bottom: Clifford Skarstedt/CP Photo Archive; Page 59: Ian Martens/CP Photo Archive; Page 60: Courtesy of Robert Davidson; Page 61 Top: National Gallery of Canada, 28747. Reproduced with the permission of West Baffin Eskimo Cooperative Ltd, Cape Dorset, Nunavut, Bottom: The Owl, drawing, 1969 by Kenojuak Ashevak,Canadian Museum of Civilization, S89-1736. Reproduced with the permission of West Baffin Eskimo Cooperative Ltd, Cape Dorset, Nunavut; Page 62: Spirits Emerge, stencil, 1987 by Kingmeata Etidlooie. Reproduced with the permission of West Baffin Eskimo Cooperative Ltd, Cape Dorset, Nunavut; Page 63: Courtesy of David Ruben Piqtoukun; Page 64: Dancing Spirits, etching/aquatint, 2003 by Sarni Pootoogook. Reproduced with the permission of West Baffin Eskimo Cooperative Ltd, Cape Dorset, Nunavut.

Reviewers

Kathryn Brownell, Terry Fox School, Toronto, Ontario

Manny Calisto,West St. Paul School, West St. Paul, Manitoba

Greer Coe, Montague Intermediate School, Montague, Prince Edward Island

Rick Elliott, John Buchan School, Toronto, Ontario

Sheri Epstein, Langstaff High School, Thornhill, Ontario

Christine Greene, Avalon East School Board, St. John's, Newfoundland

Joanne Wheeler, St. Margaret School, Calgary, Alberta